COLLINS

Toddler Bedtime

Illustrated by Sam Williams

PictureLions

An Imprint of HarperCollinsPublishers

If you enjoy TODDLER BEDTIME,
you'll love TODDLER PLAYTIME too!

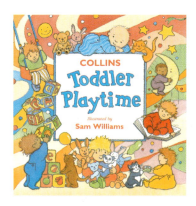

Available in hardback

First published in hardback in Great Britain by HarperCollins Publishers Ltd in 1998

First published in Picture Lions in 1998

3 5 7 9 10 8 6 4 2

ISBN: 0 00 664659-X

Picture Lions is an imprint of the Children's Division, part of HarperCollins Publishers Ltd,

77-85 Fulham Palace Road, Hammersmith, London W6 8JB.

Compilation copyright © HarperCollins Publishers Ltd 1998

Illustrations copyright © Sam Williams 1998

Text copyright, as follows:

Are You Asleep, Rabbit? © Julia Barton & Alison Campbell 1990

Into the Bath, Rosie!, Night, Night, Rosie! © Tony Bradman 1998

Mammy's Lullaby © Trish Cooke 1998

Just a Minute... © Vivian French 1998

Ten in a Bed's Too Many © Rose Impey 1998

What If? © Leon Rosselson 1998

Bathroom Boogie © Ian Whybrow 1998

The authors and illustrator assert the moral right to be identified as the authors and illustrator of the work.

A CIP catalogue record for this title is available from the British Library.

Printed in Singapore by Imago

CONTENTS

POLLY PUT THE KETTLE ON

Polly put the kettle on,
Polly put the kettle on,
Polly put the kettle on,
We'll all have tea.

Sukey take it off again,
Sukey take it off again,
Sukey take it off again,
They've all gone away.

Blow the fire and make the toast,
Put the muffins on to roast,
Who is going to eat the most?
We'll all have tea.

PAT-A-CAKE, PAT-A-CAKE!

Pat-a-cake, pat-a-cake, baker's man!
Bake me a cake as fast as you can;
Pat it and prick it and mark it with 'B'
And put it in the oven for baby and me.

INTO THE BATH, ROSIE!

Rosie's standing by the bath,
She's making lots of noise;
She can't wait to splish and splosh
And play with all her toys.

   Now she's being lifted in,
   The water's nice and warm...
   Rosie sails her little boat,
   But wait – here comes a storm!

Rosie smacks the water...
She throws a flannel – splat!
She makes a nest of bubbles,
And she wears a bubble hat!

Rosie does some swimming...
Hey, what's that glug glug glug?
Bye bye bubbles! Bye bye bath!
Rosie's pulled the plug!

Tony Bradman

JUST A MINUTE...
by Vivian French

Nikki woke up early.

"MUM!" she called. "Mum! Can I go downstairs? I want to paint a picture."

"I'll get up in a minute," Mum said sleepily. Nikki went back into her bedroom.

"I'm a great big bear asleep in its cave," she said, and she rolled herself up in her duvet. Dad looked round her door.

"Coming downstairs now?" he asked.

"Grrrrr!" Nikki growled. It was very hot in the bear's cave. Nikki climbed out and went to find Dad.

"Do you know where my paintbox is?" she asked. Dad was changing Sam's nappy.

"I'll have a look in a minute," he said.

At breakfast, Mum spooned some porridge into Nikki's bowl.

"Porridge for bears," she said. "Goodness – aren't you dressed yet?"

Nikki was searching in her toy cupboard.

"I'm looking for my paints," she said. "I think they're in here."

After breakfast, Nikki asked, "Can I do my painting now? Can I have some paper?"

Mum was feeding Sam. "Ask Dad," she said. But Dad was looking for his car keys.

"Give me a minute," he said.

At ten o'clock Mum put on her coat. "Shall we go to playgroup?" she asked.

"But I haven't finished my picture," said Nikki. "I'm painting a bear in his cave."

"Finish it later," said Mum, as she strapped Sam into his buggy.

There were lots of mums and dads and children in the playgroup hall. Nikki ran off to play with Rob and Kelly under the slide.

"Let's be bears!" she said.

"We're pirates," said Kelly. "You can play in a minute."

So Nikki made a tower with all the bricks. "Look! Mum! LOOK!" she called.

Mum was talking. "Hang on a minute," she said.

"Time to clear up!" said the play leader.

"I'll help," said Rob, and he knocked down Nikki's tower.

After lunch, Mum and Nikki and Sam went to the park.

Nikki and Sam took turns on the swing.

"You're flying, Sam!" said Nikki, as she pushed him. Sam shouted, "More! More!"

"We have to go in a minute," said Mum.

When they got home, it was time for tea. Nikki ate her fish fingers very quickly, and then looked hopefully at Mum.

"Can I finish my bear picture now?"

"Wait while I put Sam to bed," Mum said. "I'll only be a minute. You can help me give him a bath, if you like."

Sam had his bath, and then Nikki had a bath as well.

"OH!" she said, as she got out. "What about my picture?"

"You can finish it tomorrow morning," said Mum. 'Dad'll be home in a minute, and you ought to be in bed." Nikki was soon tucked up under her duvet.

"Will you read me a story about bears?" she asked.

"Of course," said Mum.

Dad shouted up the stairs. "Supper's ready!"

"I'm reading Nikki a story," Mum called back. "I'll only be a minute." Nikki looked at Mum and burst into tears.

"What's the matter?" Mum asked.

"It's always only minutes," Nikki sobbed. "And I want a proper story." Mum gave her a hug, and then smiled at her.

"Well, let's have a long story tonight, shall we?"

Nikki nodded.

"LOTS of minutes," she said.

"Lots of minutes it is," said Mum, opening the book.

BATHROOM BOOGIE

Baby in the bathroom, baby undressed –
This is the bit that the baby likes best:
Squeezing all the toothpaste, squirting the shampoo,
Collecting all the bath toys and dropping them down the loo.

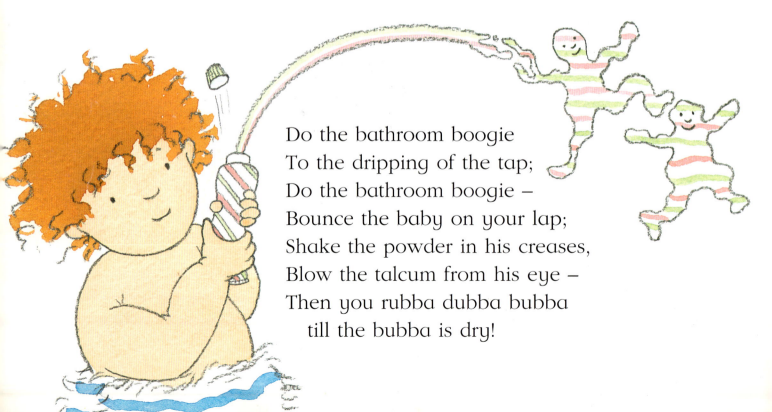

Do the bathroom boogie
To the dripping of the tap;
Do the bathroom boogie –
Bounce the baby on your lap;
Shake the powder in his creases,
Blow the talcum from his eye –
Then you rubba dubba bubba
    till the bubba is dry!

Baby in the water, baby start to cry –
Big bad soap in the baby's eye!
Never mind baby, don't you be upset –
Smack that soap, make the soap all wet!

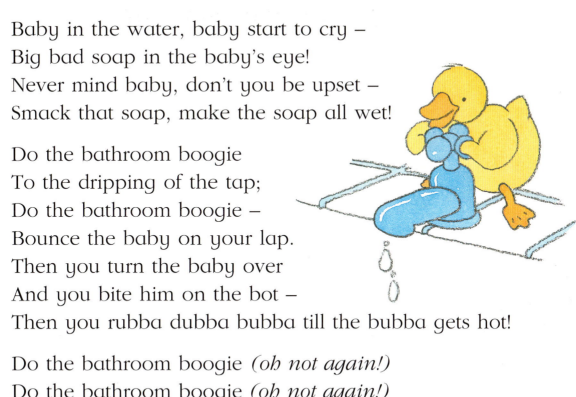

Do the bathroom boogie
To the dripping of the tap;
Do the bathroom boogie –
Bounce the baby on your lap.
Then you turn the baby over
And you bite him on the bot –
Then you rubba dubba bubba till the bubba gets hot!

Do the bathroom boogie *(oh not again!)*
Do the bathroom boogie *(oh not again!)*
Do the bathroom boogie *(oh not again!)*
            Rubba bubba
                    rubba dubba – done!

Ian Whybrow

HICKORY, DICKORY, DOCK

Hickory, dickory, dock,
The mouse ran up the clock.
The clock struck one,
The mouse ran down,
Hickory, dickory, dock.

Dickery, dickery, dare,
The pig flew up in the air.
The man in brown
Soon brought him down,
Dickery, dickery dare.

Higglety, pigglety, pop,
The dog has eaten the mop.
The pig's in a hurry,
The cat's in a flurry,
Higglety, pigglety, pop.

Fiddle-dee, diddle-dee, dee,
The cow jumped up in the tree.
The fox said, "moo",
The bat went too,
Fiddle-dee, diddle-dee, dee.

TEN IN A BED'S TOO MANY!

by Rose Impey

"Is everyone in?" said Mum.

Joshua sat up in bed to check. He counted:

1... Big Ted

2... Peanut Butter

3... Oliver

4... Chestnut

5... Special Ted

... and me.

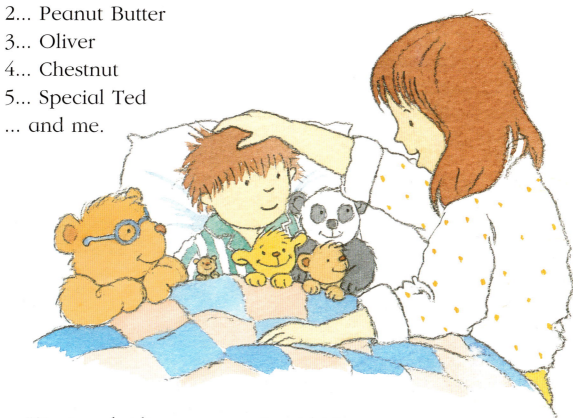

"Six in a bed's too many," said Mum.

But Joshua thought six was just right. He needed all his teddies. He couldn't sleep without them.

"Well, I'm off to work," said Mum. "Be good. Try not to bother Dad, he's tired. Now, off to sleep," she said.

But Joshua couldn't sleep. He called downstairs, "Dad, it's too dark."

Dad was dozing in his chair. But he got up and turned on the landing light.

"Is that better?" he called upstairs.

"A bit," said Joshua.

But Joshua still couldn't sleep. He called downstairs, "Dad, I'm lonely." Dad got out of his chair again and came upstairs. Max came too; his tail was wagging, his tongue was hanging out.

"How can you be lonely with all those teddies?" said Dad.

"They're all asleep," said Joshua.

"And so should you be. Here," said Dad, "Max'll keep you company."

Dad carried Max's bed in.

But Max preferred Joshua's bed. He snuggled up close.

"That's better," thought Joshua. But it wasn't. Max was no company at all. He fell asleep straight away. He started to snore. And he took up all the quilt. Joshua still couldn't sleep.

He called downstairs, "Dad, I'm cold."

Dad was dozing again, but he came upstairs.

"Let's have a cuddle," he said. "That'll warm you up." He lay down beside Joshua. But Dad was so tired he fell asleep too. Then he started to snore. It kept Joshua awake.

Joshua sat up in bed. He counted:

    1... 2... 3... 4... 5 teddies, 1 dog and Dad and Joshua.

Now there were eight in the bed.

Eight was far too many.

    Then his baby
brother came in.
Sam rubbed his eyes.

    "Where's Mummy?" he said.

    "She's at work," said Joshua. "Go back to bed."

    "I'm scared," said Sam. "I want to be in your bed."

    "There's no room," said Joshua. But Sam got in anyway.
And he brought Wibbly-Wobbly with him.

    Straightaway Sam closed his eyes, put in his thumb and fell

asleep. Max was snoring, Dad was snoring and Sam was sucking his thumb. And Joshua still couldn't get to sleep.

Joshua sat up in bed. He counted:

1... 2... 3... 4... 5 teddies, 1 dog, Dad, Sam, Wibbly-Wobbly and Joshua.

Joshua was squashed up. It was too noisy. And he still felt lonely.

"Ten in a bed is definitely too many!" said Joshua.

So Joshua got up, very carefully so that he wouldn't wake anyone. He took Special Ted with him and got into Max's bed. It was just big enough for two. Joshua snuggled down.

"That's better," he said.

"Now, go to sleep, Ted," he said. "No snoring, no thumb-sucking and no taking all the quilt."

Ted lay very quietly and went to sleep as good as gold. Joshua was just dropping off too, when Mum came home. She peeped round the door. She couldn't believe her eyes.

"Oh, Joshua," she said. "Whatever's going on in here and what are you doing in the dog's bed?"

But Joshua said, "Shhh, we're all asleep."

NIGHT, NIGHT, ROSIE!

Rosie's climbing up the stairs,
It's time to go to bed,
Time to find her nightie
And her favourite ted.

Rosie wants a story
And a game or two...
Ride a cock-horse to Banbury Cross!
And lots of... peekaboo!

In your cot now, Rosie,
Snuggle down, sleep tight.
Kiss, kiss, kiss for Rosie...
And one for ted – night, night!

But Rosie isn't tired...
She just wants to play.
Life with Rosie's never dull,
It's full of fun each day!

Tony Bradman

ARE YOU ASLEEP, RABBIT?

by Alison Campbell and Julia Barton

One night it snowed. Rabbit was very cold outside in her hutch.

"You'd better come inside," said Donald.

He found some newspapers and a grocery box for a bed, and put Rabbit in. Then Donald blew Rabbit a goodnight kiss and crept up to bed.

But Donald could not sleep.

"Is Rabbit cold?" he thought.
He crept downstairs with his fluffy pink blanket.

"Are you asleep, Rabbit?" he said.

But Rabbit wasn't asleep. She was dancing in and out of the table legs.

"Just one dance, Rabbit, then you really must go to bed," said Donald. And they danced a midnight dance.

Hoppity skip past the sink. Hoppity skip round the vegetable rack. Hoppity jump over the brush until...

they were so tired they had to stop.

Donald said goodnight again, and tiptoed up to bed.
But Donald could not sleep.

"Does Rabbit want a drink?" he thought.

Donald filled his shiny green mug with water to take
downstairs to Rabbit.

"Are you asleep, Rabbit?" said Donald.

But Rabbit wasn't asleep. She was under the sink nibbling
a packet of soap powder.

"Rabbit! Don't eat that!" said Donald. "Look, I've brought
you a drink."

Rabbit woffled her little white nose and lapped up all the water. Donald said goodnight again, and tiptoed up to bed.

But Donald still could not sleep.
Mummy was asleep.
Teddy was asleep. But...

"Is Rabbit asleep?" thought Donald.

He carried his softest pillow down to Rabbit.

"Are you asleep, Rabbit?" said Donald. But Rabbit still wasn't asleep. The fridge door was open and Rabbit was eating the tomatoes.

"Oh Rabbit, I can't leave you alone at all," said Donald.

He made a bed under the table with the fluffy blanket and the pillow. Then he picked Rabbit up gently and tucked her in beside him.

"Now I'll be able to keep an eye on you, Rabbit," said Donald.

He stroked her ears over and over until she closed her eyes.

"Goodnight, Rabbit," said Donald, and they both fell fast asleep.

HUSH, LITTLE BABY

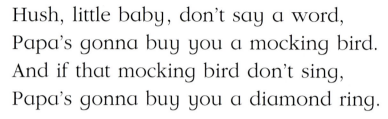

Hush, little baby, don't say a word,
Papa's gonna buy you a mocking bird.
And if that mocking bird don't sing,
Papa's gonna buy you a diamond ring.

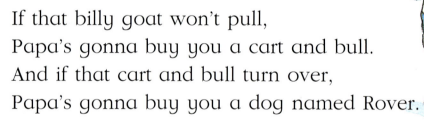

If that diamond ring turns brass,
Papa's gonna buy you a looking glass.
And if that looking glass gets broke,
Papa's gonna buy you a billy goat.

If that billy goat won't pull,
Papa's gonna buy you a cart and bull.
And if that cart and bull turn over,
Papa's gonna buy you a dog named Rover.

And if that dog named Rover won't bark,
Papa's gonna buy you a horse and cart.
And if that horse and cart fall down,
You'll still be the sweetest little baby in town.

WHAT IF?

by Leon Rosselson

"Mum! Come here, Mum! Come and sit with me. I can't sleep and I'm scared of the dark and there's something horrible under the bed."

"Hush, my love. There's nothing at all to be frightened of and there's nothing and nobody under the bed, but I'll sit with you if you like till you go to sleep."

"Can we play, Mum? Can we play a game?"

"It's late, my love, it's late and I'm tired and you should be asleep."

"Just one game, Mum. One game of What If?"

"All right, then. One game of What If? and after that you must close your eyes and go to sleep."

"I'm closing my eyes now. I'm thinking. What if – ? What if I changed to a bird and what if I flew away high, high to the top of the sky? Would you be sad?"

"If you were a bird, a little brown bird, I'd sing you a song to call you home and when you flew down, I'd stroke your feathery wings so you'd know, my bird, my little brown flyaway bird, that I love you still."

"But, Mum, what if tomorrow I woke up and found I was tall as a tree, like a giant, a big clumsy giant and what if I ate up all of the biscuits and cakes? Would you be cross?"

"If you were a giant, a hungry giant, I'd sit you, tall as you were, on my knee and feed you the biggest jam sandwich that's ever been seen so you'd know, my giant, my tall-as-a-treetop giant, that I love you still."

"And what if I turned into – What can I be? I know – a monster with big hairy feet and a tail and a nose like a mushroom and ears that stick up like the ears of a wolf? Would you be scared?"

"If you were a monster, a hairy monster, I'd kiss you one, two, three times three on your mushroom nose so you'd know, my monster, my strange and funny old monstery one, that I love you still."

"What if I was a monkey and did naughty things like climb up the curtains and spill all the milk and make a mess everywhere? Would you tell me off?"

"If you were a monkey, a mischievous monkey, I'd lift you up and throw you into the air and tickle you here and tickle you there so you'd know, my monkey, my never-stop-chattering monkey, that I love you still."

"What if I was a baby again? What if I couldn't talk? What if I sucked my thumb when I was tired, when I was ever so, ever so tired...? What if...?"

"Sleep, my love,
my baby,
my monkey,
my monster,
my giant,
my little
brown bird.

Sweet dreams."

MAMMY'S LULLABY

Oh

Why you cry so

Why you fighting – fighting

Eyes wide open
Why you fighting sleep so?

It time to sleep now

Close those tired eyes now

Rest yourself
and save yourself

For the morning light now

Nobody ever tell you
Not to walk against the wind

Eh

Nobody ever tell you
That the night time is your friend

So

Why you cry so
Why you fighting – fighting

Eyes wide open
Why you fighting sleep so?

It time to sleep now
Hush a little
Sigh now
Cos it sweet now
Yes
To sleep now
Yesssssssssssssss
ssssssssssssleep.

Trish Cooke

TWINKLE, TWINKLE, LITTLE STAR

Twinkle, twinkle, little star,
How I wonder what you are!
Up above the world so high,
Like a diamond in the sky.

When the blazing sun is gone,
When he nothing shines upon,
Then you show your little light,
Twinkle, twinkle, all the night.

Then the traveller in the dark,
Thanks you for your tiny spark,
He could not see which way to go,
If you did not twinkle so.

In the dark blue sky you keep,
And often through my curtains peep,
For you never shut your eye,
Till the sun is in the sky.

As your bright and tiny spark,
Lights the traveller in the dark –
Though I know not what you are,
Twinkle, twinkle, little star.